THE POWER OF THE PAUSE

TOOLS FOR RESTORING BALANCE IN A BUSY WORLD

MARCIE STRAHAN, ED.D.

Copyright © 2025 Marcie Strahan

All rights reserved. No part of this book may be used or reproduced by any means, graphic, electronic, or mechanical, including photocopying recording, taping, or by any information storage retrieval system, without the written permission of the publisher except in the case of brief quotations embodied in critical articles and reviews.

Dedication

This book is dedicated to every person who has ever felt tired, overwhelmed, or pressured to keep going when their body and spirit were asking for a pause. May these pages remind you that grace is not failure and you are worthy of slowing down.

Acknowledgements

This book exists because of the people who held space for me. Sometimes the space was held knowingly, and sometimes quietly, without me even realizing it. To those who thought of me, spoke my name in rooms I was not in, and elevated my voice to share a message of self-care and well-being, thank you.

To my loving husband, inspiring mother, DTDSTT crew, and amazing Choc Doc sisters, thank you for your patience, love, and constant reminders that rest is a necessity. Your support gave me the freedom to slow down, listen to my own voice, and capture my message in these pages.

I am especially grateful to the mentors, colleagues, and communities who challenged me to think differently about success, productivity, and purpose. You reminded me that alignment matters more than achievement and that pausing can be a powerful act of leadership.

Finally, to every reader who has ever felt guilty for resting or questioned their worth in moments of stillness, thank you for choosing yourself. May this book serve as a gentle companion on your journey toward balance, clarity, wholeness, and the moment of grace found in the moments where you permit yourself to pause.

Table of Contents

Introduction - The Pause That Changed Everything 06

How to Use This Book 12

How to Use The Activities 14

Part I: Pause - The Art of Stopping with Purpose 15
Chapter 1: The World Keeps on Turning
Chapter 2: Permission to Pause
Chapter 3: Creating a Sacred Space to Stop

Part II: Breathe - Be Present in the Moment 33
Chapter 4: Breathing Through the Busy
Chapter 5: Mindfulness in Motion
Chapter 6: The Body Remembers

Part 3: Proceed - Moving Forward with Intention 51
Chapter 7: Proceed with Purpose
Chapter 8: Rest as Resistance
Chapter 9: Grace for the Journey

Part 4: Living in the Pause 71
Chapter 10: The Pause in Community
Chapter 11: From Practice to Lifestyle

Conclusion - The Power Within the Pause 85

The Pause That Changed Everything

The world keeps turning when you pause. The miracle is that you return to it stronger, clearer, and more whole.

I remember sitting in a Youth Mental Health First Aid training, multitasking as always, but still tuned in to the facilitator's delivery. My section was coming up next, so I was listening… ok, half-listening, and also wrapping up the task in front of me.

Anywho… it was at that moment when the facilitator asked the group, "When did you realize that self-care is necessary?"

She had my full attention. At that moment, my stomach dropped because if she called on me, I wasn't sure I could get the words out. Everyone who knows me knows I am passionate about advocating for self-care. I've incorporated practices here and there, but I don't think I ever stated the reason for the pivot and the necessity of self-care to make sure I continued showing up as the best version of myself. When she asked me the question and patiently waited for my response, I remembered the moment when everything shifted.

Let me tell you my Sophia story. Picture it, Houston, 2009. My life came to a sudden halt.

I had just undergone a major surgery to address a health condition. I'd prepared for the surgery physically. I signed the papers, cleared my schedule, followed every pre-op instruction, but I had not prepared emotionally. How could I?

I personally knew someone who faced complications from the same procedure. I remembered the panic in my chest as I ran to her hospital bedside, surrounded by machines, prayers, and fear. The news had been grim, and our circle had already begun preparing for the possibility that we might lose her.

So when my doctor told me the surgery was inevitable, the decision was clear, but so was the weight of what I was walking into. I carried her story with me. I carried the memory of those hospital hallways and the quiet truth that I would need to make time for my own physical and emotional healing. I told myself I'd rest properly. I told myself I'd slow down.

The doctor's orders were loud, clear, and simple: Rest. Not "slow down a little," not "take it easy." Rest. Fully. Completely without room for negotiations.

So there I was at home, wrapped in blankets and discomfort, forced into a stillness I never would have chosen on my own. My body insisted on rest, and for once, I had no choice but to listen.

It was a quiet morning. I lay there, sore and still, letting The Young and the Restless play as a familiar distraction. In the middle of my wondering how many times Victor and Nikki would break up, rekindle, and remarry, the show cut away. A red banner flashed across the screen announcing Breaking News, and something in me stilled, sensing the moment carried weight.

Then the news dropped, Michael Jackson had died at fifty years old.

News anchors scrambled for updates, social media erupted, and my phone began buzzing with notifications. In that moment, I was in shock, sore from the procedure, and struggling to process it all.

I stared at the television, frozen not just at the loss of a global icon, but at the surreal experience of watching everyone continue while I remained in stillness that I didn't ask for. In that forced pause, I realized something profound: Even while I rested, the world kept turning.

Life didn't stop just because I was recovering.

Emails still went out. Meetings still happened. People lived, loved, celebrated, and mourned. Life moved on without me having to carry it.

I began to see self-care not as a luxury or indulgence, but as a fundamental necessity, embracing sustainable habits that nourish the body, empower the mind, and sustain the soul. Pausing. Breathing. Allowing myself space meant I was showing up as my best self in every area of life.

This book is about reclaiming the pause. It's about giving yourself the space and opportunity to breathe. It's about being intentional in your approach. Together, we will explore how self-care can become an essential, accessible part of your life, not just for you, but for the communities and spaces you influence.

REFLECTION QUESTIONS

- Recall a moment when you were forced to pause. What did you learn about yourself during that time?

- Who or what in your life benefits when you prioritize your rest, boundaries, and self-care?

How to Use This Book

This book is meant to be more than something you read. It is a companion for your journey. It invites you to pause, breathe, and move forward with intention in your everyday life. As you begin, there is nothing you need to fix, change, or accomplish. Simply notice. Let the words meet you where you are, and engage with them in a way that honors your rhythm, your schedule, and your needs.

- **Read with Presence, Not Pressure**
    - You don't have to finish it in one sitting. Take your time.
    - Treat this book as a companion for your journey, not a checklist to complete.

- **Pause at Each Chapter or Section**
    - Use the pauses embedded in the text to reflect on your experiences, emotions, and priorities.
    - Highlight phrases, make notes, or journal your thoughts.

- **Practice the Reflection Prompts**
    - Each chapter includes prompts designed to deepen your awareness and help you apply insights to your life.
    - Answer honestly. These reflections are for you.

- **Integrate the Mini Practices**
    - Small, intentional habits matter more than occasional grand gestures.
    - Use the exercises and suggested practices to anchor mindfulness, self-care, and intentional action into your day.

- **Return Often**
    - Life moves fast, and moments of overwhelm will come. This book is meant to be revisited whenever you need a reset.
    - Each read may reveal new insights or a different perspective, depending on where you are in your journey.

- **Share the Pause**
    - While this is a personal journey, self-care also creates ripples. Share insights, stories, or practices with others who may benefit.
    - Model the pause and inspire those around you to reclaim their own time and energy.

How to Use the Activities

To fully benefit from the activities at the end of each chapter, approach them with intention and openness. You can complete activities sequentially, skip to the ones that resonate most, or revisit favorites whenever you need grounding. The key is consistency. These exercises are not tasks to check off, but tools to help you cultivate awareness, balance, and a deeper connection to your well-being.

KEY POINTS

Throughout the book, highlighted key points summarize the main ideas. They serve as a quick reference to reinforce the lessons and encourage you to apply what you've learned. Use them as prompts to take action and integrate sustainable self-care habits into your daily life.

PAUSE PRACTICE

Simple activities are provided throughout the book. These activities are designed to help you reconnect with yourself throughout your day. These practices are gentle invitations to create pockets of stillness, clarity, and intention. You can use them in the way that you think is most helpful to you.

REFLECTION QUESTIONS

The reflection questions are designed to help you process and apply the insights from each chapter to your own life. Your responses are for you and your growth. Use these questions to notice patterns, uncover insights, and identify actionable steps that support your well-being.

PAUSE
The Art of Stopping
with Purpose

> *Stopping with purpose allows us to respond instead of react, and to lead from a grounded place.*

01 The World Keeps on Turning

"A moment of stillness can shift a day, a mindset, and a community."

Life moves fast. Too fast, sometimes. Society tells us to keep up or risk being left behind. We convince ourselves that stopping is dangerous and pausing is a sign of weakness, or worse, procrastination. But the truth is the opposite: pausing is a form of strength.

Burnout is real!
Fatigue, emotional depletion, and chronic stress become impossible to ignore.

In case you've ever wondered, when you reach this point, it is indeed a wake-up call: the relentless pursuit of busyness steals your well-being. You may not always be fortunate enough to have a colleague who will smile at you and say, "Take a breath." I'm glad I did, and I'm grateful I dared to pause.

My colleague's directive stopped me in my tracks. I literally put down my pen, closed my eyes, and did exactly as told...

I took a breath. One long, intentional breath... and then another.

A pause that steadies the nervous system, softens the shoulders, and creates just enough space to respond instead of react. Sometimes that's the work, choosing presence, even for two breaths. Within those moments, the tension drained from my shoulders, the chatter in my mind quieted, and a sense of clarity returned. And in that clarity, I realized something essential:

If you don't pause, you can't lead yourself, and you certainly can't lead others.

Pausing is not optional; it is necessary. It's when we step off the hamster wheel long enough to see clearly, understand our direction, and make intentional choices about how we move forward. While this may sound like common sense, many of us struggle with the same tension between constant motion and meaningful reflection.

Pausing begins with permission, and that is where the next chapter begins.

PAUSE PRACTICE

- Begin by noticing the tension in your body. Without judgment, scan for areas where tension may be lingering. Where are you holding stress? Is it in your shoulders, jaw, neck, or lower back? Simply observe where stress is being held.

- Gently close your eyes, or soften your gaze if closing your eyes does not feel comfortable. Allow your attention to turn inward.

- Inhale slowly through your nose for four counts, letting the breath expand your chest and belly. Hold the breath gently for four counts. Then exhale through your mouth for six counts, releasing any tightness you may feel.

- Repeat this breathing pattern three times. As you do, notice the subtle shifts in your body and mind. Notice your shoulders softening, your thoughts slowing, or your breath becoming steadier. When you are ready, open your eyes and carry this sense of calm with you as you move forward.

REFLECTION QUESTIONS

- What are the signs your body and mind give you when you need to pause?
- How could pausing change the way you respond to stress today?

02

Permission to Pause

Somewhere along the way, we learned to believe that rest must be earned.

You don't need permission to pause.

You need grace.
You need acceptance.
You need to allow the pause to hold you, not judge you.

For years, I confused being busy with being purposeful. My husband often refers to this as a "Marcie Day."

My calendar was full, my days were packed, and my energy was stretched to the limit. I was always doing something, always needed somewhere, always responding to someone else's crisis while internalizing it as my own. From the outside, it looked productive. On the inside, it felt draining. Busyness kept me moving, but it didn't always move me forward. Purpose, on the other hand, feels different.

Purpose is intentional and aligned. It allows for rest because it understands sustainability. It knows that constant motion without reflection leads to burnout, not fulfillment.

One of the hardest lessons I had to learn was how to say no, especially when everything in me wanted to say yes. There were moments when the invitation sounded exciting, the opportunity seemed important, and the expectations felt heavy. Saying yes felt easier than explaining myself. Easier than disappointing someone. Easier than sitting with the discomfort of choosing myself.

I remember one specific moment when my body was exhausted, my mind was overwhelmed, and my spirit was quietly asking for rest. Still, I reached for my phone, ready to say yes out of habit. But I paused. I took a breath. Instead of responding automatically, I asked myself one honest question: What do I actually need right now?

The answer wasn't another commitment. It was rest. So I said no. Not dramatically. Not defensively. Just clearly.

It wasn't easy, but I learned how to be honest with myself and honor my needs.

Permitting yourself to pause means releasing the need to justify your rest. You don't owe anyone an explanation for taking care of yourself.

Rest doesn't require a reason, and grace doesn't need permission.

Unlearning hustle culture makes room for wholeness. We begin to understand that slowing down isn't quitting; it's a way to move forward. Slowing down is choosing sustainability. It's choosing presence. It's choosing yourself.

Permission to pause is not about doing less for the sake of doing less. It's about creating space to breathe, to reflect, and to move forward with clarity.

- The pause is powerful because it creates perspective. The world continues even when you stop; your pause does not halt life, it clarifies it.

- Stillness isn't the absence of action; forced or intentional, the pause is the foundation for meaningful and deliberate action.

✦ PAUSE PRACTICE

Let's practice permitting yourself to rest without guilt, justification, or productivity attached.

Pause & Breathe
Take a moment to ground yourself. Take three slow, deep breaths. After breathing, describe how your body feels right now:

Notice the Pressure
What are you feeling pressured to do, respond to, or complete right now?

Check In With Yourself
What do you actually need in this moment?
(Examples: rest, clarity, space, support, quiet)

Release the Guilt
What thoughts or beliefs make it hard for you to pause without guilt?

Offer Yourself Permission
Write a permission statement to yourself beginning with:
"I give myself permission to…"

Choose the Next Step
What is one intentional choice you can make after this pause, whether rest or action?

Affirmation
"I permit myself to pause. I do not need to earn rest."

03 Creating a Sacred Space to Stop

Pausing does not require a retreat or a complete life reset. Often, it begins with a small, intentional space within the place you already call home. The environments we move through each day shape our energy, our focus, and our ability to slow down.

The sacred space supports mental well-being, reduces stress, and encourages mindful moments that strengthen resilience. Most importantly, it reminds you that you deserve spaces that nurture your peace, honor your voice, and make room for the stillness required to move with intention through the rest of your day.

This chapter explores how thoughtfully creating space at home can become a daily invitation to pause, breathe, and reconnect with yourself. Even small changes can make a meaningful difference in how you feel.

Tips for Creating a Pause Space

Creating a pause space is about more than where you sit; it's about how you show up. When you intentionally carve out a small sanctuary, you signal to your mind and body that rest, reflection, and restoration are priorities, not luxuries. This sacred space can be indoors or outdoors, and it becomes a grounding ritual: a place where clarity rises, creativity flows, and emotional balance is restored.

Create a Physical Space

Choose a designated corner or spot in your home or workspace that signals rest. This doesn't need to be large or elaborate. A chair by a window, a small table, or a quiet corner is enough. Add elements that invite calm: soft lighting, a candle, a journal, a plant, or any object that brings you a sense of ease. Comfortable seating matters; this space should gently tell your body it is safe to slow down.

Cultivate Emotional Space

Just as important as the physical environment is the emotional one. Bring intention to how you protect your energy by setting boundaries, communicating your needs clearly, and releasing the pressure to always be available or productive. Emotional space also means allowing yourself moments of grace, accepting where you are without judgment, and honoring your needs.

Let the Space Evolve

Your pause space is not meant to be perfect or permanent. It can change with seasons, moods, and needs. What matters most is that it remains a place, both physically and emotionally, where you give yourself permission to pause and be present.

Practical Ways to Make Room for Pause

Morning Rituals

Start your day with a grounding practice: a slow stretch, a moment of gratitude, a cup of tea without checking emails, repeating a simple affirmation, journaling, or reading a daily devotion. A gentle morning routine sets the tone for how you show up throughout the day.

Solitude

Even brief moments alone can recharge your emotional and mental energy. Solitude allows you to hear your own thoughts, make sense of your feelings, and give yourself space to breathe. These moments can be enhanced through simple sensory rituals, such as using calming fragrances like lavender, sandalwood, or cedarwood, which help signal your mind and body to slow down and settle into stillness.

Technology Boundaries

Silencing notifications, establishing "no phone zones," or setting aside a time each evening to unplug can help protect your peace. The intentional boundaries you set quiet the loudness of technology.

The Power of Mini-Pauses

Sometimes, two minutes of stillness is enough to reset your energy and return to the best version of yourself. Mini-pauses can look like taking a deep breath before entering a meeting, driving without the radio playing, practicing intentional breathwork at a red light, slowly sipping coffee on the patio, or sitting in the driveway for a few quiet minutes after work before entering the house. These mini-pauses throughout the day help you recenter and regain clarity. Being intentional about these moments, before stress builds and frustration boils over, can make the difference between responding with purpose and reacting in ways that lead to undesired consequences.

 KEY POINTS

- Sacred space begins with intention. You need a purposeful space for peace.

- Stillness shifts your energy. Quiet moments help you hear what your body, mind, and spirit are trying to tell you.

PAUSE PRACTICE

This guided morning ritual helps you start your day grounded, present, and connected to your needs before the demands of the day take over.

Step 1: Arrive
Pause before reaching for your phone or beginning your tasks.
- Take three slow, deep breaths
- Place one hand on your chest or stomach
- With each exhale, release urgency

Step 2: Ground
Bring awareness to the present moment.
- Notice your physical sensations (tension, ease, fatigue, energy)
- Notice your emotional state without judgment

Step 3: Set an Intention
Choose one word or phrase to guide your day.
Examples: calm, focus, grace, patience, ease, clarity

Step 4: Gentle Action
Choose one small act that supports your well-being.
- Stretch or move gently
- Drink water or tea mindfully
- Light a candle
- Write one sentence in your journal
- Sit quietly for a moment

Step 5: Begin with Grace
Before moving into your day, read or repeat quietly:

I don't have to rush to be worthy.
I am allowed to move through this day with intention.

BREATHE
Be Present in the Moment

> *Presence is the gift we give ourselves*
> *before we offer anything to others.*

04 Breathing Through the Busy

"It's not the load that breaks you down, it's the way you carry it."
Lou Holtz

Stress is a natural part of life, but how we respond physiologically, emotionally, and mentally determines its impact. Mindful breathing and intentional pauses give us the tools to carry life's demands with greater resilience, clarity, and calm.

When we experience stress, both body and mind respond. Physiologically, stress activates the sympathetic nervous system (SNS), triggering the release of cortisol. This increases heart rate, respiratory rate, and blood pressure. Stress responses can be immediate or delayed, acute or chronic. Heightened SNS activity in response to psychological stress is pro-inflammatory, contributing to both mental and physical health risks. Chronic stress is a major factor in conditions such as cardiovascular disease, cancer, anxiety, and depression.

Mindful, deep breathing offers a powerful counterbalance. Research shows that intentional breathing activates the parasympathetic nervous system, lowering heart rate, reducing cortisol levels, and promoting relaxation (Harvard Health Publishing, 2020; American Psychological Association, 2019). Regular practice supports emotional regulation, enhances focus, and improves overall well-being. Calm is contagious: when you model steady breathing, those around you are more likely to feel centered and responsive.

Under normal circumstances, breathing is automatic and largely unnoticed, at least until something goes wrong.

As a certified yoga teacher and social-emotional learning facilitator, I view breath as a bridge between our internal and external realities.

Each inhale brings in what we need from our environment, and each exhale releases what no longer serves us.

The state of our breathing is intimately tied to our nervous system and, in turn, to our experience of ourselves. Deep, full breaths send calming signals to the brain, while rapid, shallow breaths signal distress.

The beauty of this connection is that because we can observe, accept, and create our breathing, we can use it as an access point to better observe, accept, and influence our state of mind. Simple practices like box breathing, 4-7-8 breathing, or pausing for three deep breaths during a stressful moment can reset the nervous system and bring clarity to our responses.

I'll never forget a staff meeting a few years ago when tensions were running high. A colleague disagreed with a process I had put in place, and I could feel my chest tighten and my thoughts racing as the action stirred up dissent within the team. Usually, my instinct would have been to respond immediately, perhaps defensively, and even heatedly.

Instead, I paused. I took one slow, deliberate breath, letting it fill my lungs, then I exhaled fully. That single breath created a fraction of space between my reaction and my response. I noticed my heart rate slow, and my mind was clear, just enough to choose my words carefully. When I finally spoke, my tone was calm and measured. I acknowledged their perspective, clarified my own, and we found a solution that honored both viewpoints. That moment taught me a valuable lesson: One intentional breath can shift the energy in a room, improve communication, and prevent unnecessary conflict.

The state of our breath is one of the most powerful tools we have for managing stress and increasing self-awareness. Consistent use of mindful breathing improves resilience, reduces emotional reactivity, and positively influences the emotional climate around us. Calm is contagious; by breathing intentionally, we help others practice mindfulness and breathe easier, too.

Benefits of Deep Breathing

Deep breathing supports both physical health and emotional well-being by calming the body's stress response. Research shows that intentional breathing can lower heart rate and blood pressure, reduce psychological and physiological stress, and ease symptoms of anxiety and depression. It also supports respiratory health and improves quality of life for individuals managing chronic conditions when practiced alongside medical care.

Beyond these physical effects, deep breathing activates the parasympathetic nervous system, promoting relaxation, emotional regulation, and mental clarity. Regular practice improves focus, energy, and resilience by enhancing oxygen exchange and supporting healthy brain and metabolic function. Together, these benefits make mindful breathing a simple yet powerful tool for restoring balance and sustaining well-being.

✦ PAUSE PRACTICE

Breathe in gently through your nose for 4 seconds, hold your breath for 7 seconds, and breathe out forcefully through your mouth for 8 seconds. Repeat for 4 breath cycles max for the first month, then go up to 8 (but no more than two sets of 8 a day).

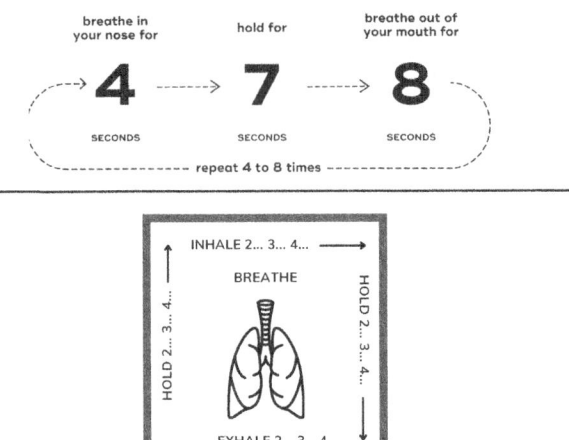

Use your finger to slowly trace a path around the square. Focus on your breath by slowly inhaling, holding, and exhaling for a four-second count. Repeat as needed until you feel calm and centered.

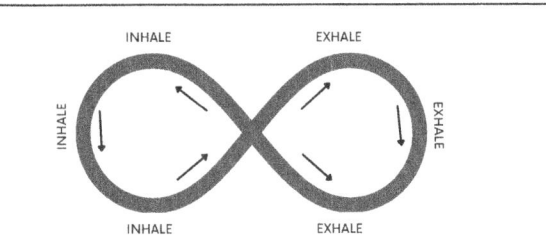

Start in the middle, go up to the left while inhaling and holding your breath. When you get to the middle, slowly exhale and trace the right side of the figure. Focus on your breath while tracing the figure with your finger. Repeat as needed until you feel calm.

05 Mindfulness in Motion

Mindfulness is often misunderstood as something that requires stillness, silence, or extra time carved out of an already full day. In reality, mindfulness is not a task to add to your list; it is a way of moving through life with awareness. It is less about doing more and more and more about noticing what is already happening.

Mindfulness as a lifestyle means learning to be present in motion. It lives in the ordinary moments that make up your day: walking from one space to another, preparing a meal, journaling a few thoughts, driving to work, teaching a lesson, leading a meeting, or having a conversation. These moments do not require perfection or performance. They simply invite attention.

It's easy to move through life on autopilot. Consider the following weekly activities: folding laundry while watching television, planning the next task while completing the current one, or replaying yesterday while rushing into tomorrow.

In doing so, we often miss what is happening in the present moment: how our body feels, what our breath is doing, or the small signs of beauty along our path. Mindfulness gently brings us back.

When you move mindfully, you begin to notice the rhythm of your steps, the warmth of your hands, the tone of your voice, and the pace of your breath. Presence grounds you in what is happening now rather than pulling you into anticipation, worry, or distraction. It reconnects you to your body and your lived experience.

At its core, mindfulness is the practice of intentionally paying attention to the present moment without judgment. While its roots come from ancient contemplative traditions, mindfulness has also been widely studied and shown to support stress reduction, emotional regulation, physical health, and overall well-being. Practicing mindfulness has been linked with improvements in everyday well-being and deeper emotional connections with others, as well as positive changes in health attitudes and behaviors.

Gratitude serves as a powerful anchor for mindfulness in motion. When you intentionally acknowledge what is going well, even in small, routine moments, you interrupt the rush and reconnect with meaning.

Gratitude does not deny challenges; it reframes your focus. It reminds you that even in the midst of responsibility and movement, there is something steady to appreciate. Over time, practicing gratitude trains your attention to notice presence instead of pressure and abundance instead of absence. It softens your inner dialogue, strengthens emotional resilience, and creates space for joy to coexist with effort. In this way, gratitude becomes more than a feeling; it becomes a grounding practice that keeps you connected to what matters most as you move through your day.

Mindfulness also invites acceptance. It teaches you to notice thoughts, emotions, and sensations as they arise without labeling them as good or bad. Some moments may feel calm, while others may feel uncomfortable or restless. The practice is not about forcing relaxation but about staying present with whatever is happening and responding with kindness toward yourself.

As mindfulness becomes part of your daily rhythm, it begins to change how you experience your life. You may notice that you savor small joys more easily, respond instead of react, and feel less consumed by regret about the past or worry about the future. Over time, these moments of awareness accumulate, transforming routine into reflection and movement into meaning.

Mindfulness allows you to live your life without feeling like you are racing through it. It softens urgency, increases clarity, and creates space for calm, even on busy days. You don't need to stop your life to be mindful. You simply need to be present within it.

As we slow down enough to pay attention, we begin to recognize that presence is not only a mental practice, but a physical one. Our bodies are constantly responding to our thoughts, emotions, and experiences, often before we fully understand them. When we move mindfully, we start to sense where tension lingers, where energy flows, and where something within us is asking to be acknowledged. This awareness gently leads us to the next truth: the body remembers what the mind may overlook, and listening to it is an essential part of the pause.

  KEY POINTS

- Every ordinary moment can become extraordinary when you're present.

- Mindfulness is a way of being, not another item on your to-do list.

- Gratitude transforms routine into reflection and awareness into meaning.

REFLECTION QUESTIONS

- What is one daily activity you can turn into a mindful ritual by slowing down, noticing your breath, and practicing gratitude?

- How might your day feel different if you approached this activity with full presence instead of rushing through it?

06 The Body Remembers

Our bodies are living archives. Every experience, whether it's joyful, stressful, or traumatic, leaves an imprint. Often, we focus on the mind, thinking we "process" emotions there, but the truth is, our bodies never forget. Tight shoulders, a racing heart, shallow breathing, or even fatigue are all messages signaling what we need in that moment. These physical sensations are not random; they are the language of your body, quietly telling you that something matters, that something needs attention.

Think about how your body reacts to stress. Maybe you notice a clenching in your jaw when you're anxious or a heaviness in your chest when you feel sadness. Perhaps your stomach twists with worry, or your muscles ache after carrying tension for days or even months without release. These sensations are more than discomfort; they are signals. Your body is reminding you that you are alive, that you have needs, and that those needs deserve recognition.

The first step toward true self-care is learning to listen. Somatic awareness is tuning into sensations in your body and giving them the space to be noticed. It requires slowing down, being present, and observing without judgment. When you train yourself to listen to your body and truly process the messages it offers, you can uncover emotions and stress you might not even be conscious of.

Pausing to notice these sensations is not indulgent; it is essential. In a world that glorifies "pushing through," permitting yourself to stop feels radical. Intuitive rest, the kind that responds to your body's rhythms rather than the clock or a to-do list, allows for genuine restoration. It is in these moments of pause that you allow yourself to replenish energy, release tension, and reconnect with your inner guidance.

This pause can take many forms. It could be a few deep breaths in the morning, a short walk outside to feel the sun on your skin, or simply closing your eyes for a few moments to notice what you feel without distraction. These small but deliberate acts are ways to honor your body and its messages.

Caring for your body is also an act of mindfulness. Sleep, hydration, nourishing food, and movement are not just physical necessities; they are invitations to reconnect with yourself.

Each act, when done with attention and intention, is a declaration of self-respect. Drinking water becomes an acknowledgment of your body's needs. A walk outside transforms into a meditation in motion. Eating a balanced meal becomes a ritual of gratitude.

Mindful nourishment is not about perfection or adhering to rigid rules. It is about attuning to what your body needs in the moment. Maybe today your body craves more rest than exercise. Perhaps it longs for a hearty, comforting meal or a quiet space to stretch and breathe. Listening and responding to these needs is a form of self-care that builds resilience, strengthens your connection to yourself, and reminds you that your body is a trusted ally.

Learning to listen to your body is not a one-time practice. It is a lifelong dialogue. The more you pay attention, the more you will understand its language, and the more you will cultivate a deeper sense of trust, compassion, and mindfulness in your life.

When we learn to listen to the body, we begin to understand its quiet wisdom. But awareness alone is not enough. What the body asks for next is not more effort; it's rest. When we learn to listen to the body, the next step is learning how to move forward without betraying it, which we dive into in the next chapter.

PAUSE PRACTICE

Body Scan Meditation
- Close your eyes and take three deep breaths.
- Starting at the top of your head, slowly bring your attention to each part of your body (forehead, jaw, neck, shoulders, arms, chest, abdomen, hips, legs, feet) while breathing.
- Notice any sensations, tightness, tingling, warmth, or discomfort, without judgment.
- Imagine releasing tension with each exhale.
- Finish by noticing how your body feels as a whole.

Intuitive Rest Check-In
- Set a timer for 2–3 minutes during the day.
- Pause and ask: What does my body need right now? Rest? Movement? Nourishment?
- Follow your body's guidance, even if it's just a few deep breaths, quick stretch, or sip of water.
- Notice how honoring these small signals changes your energy or focus.

Mindful Nourishment Practice
- Choose one meal or snack today to eat without distractions.
- Notice the colors, textures, and aromas of your food.
- Take slow, deliberate bites, paying attention to flavors and how the food makes you feel.

Sensation Journaling
- At the end of the day, reflect on the patterns.
- How can you honor the recurring signals?

PROCEED
Moving Forward with Intention

> *Self-care isn't a luxury; it's the art of creating sustainable habits that nourish your body, empower your mind, and sustain your soul.*

07 Proceed with Purpose

"Every empowered 'no' opens the door to a more intentional 'yes.'"

There comes a point on every journey when you must decide not just what to do next, but how to move. This chapter is about the shift from living on autopilot to living with alignment, from constant doing to intentional being.

So much of our lives is spent reacting. Take a moment to reflect on your previous week. Without knowing your professional title or personal commitment, I'd almost bet money that the majority of your time was spent responding to pressure, obligations, expectations, and the invisible pull of "should." Purpose asks us to pause long enough to listen.

When we create space for clarity, we begin to recognize what truly deserves our energy and what merely fills our calendar.

A conversation with a close friend revealed an important truth: **sometimes the most respectful response is a simple, unqualified "no."**

We were invited to a party. The party was hosted by a friend of ours and was being held in honor of a personal friend of hers. Neither of us was particularly connected to the guest of honor, but we felt obligated because we respected the person throwing the event.

What began as a quick text exchange turned into a full fifteen-minute back-and-forth discussion trying to justify why it was okay not to go.

"We're tired."
"It's been a long week."
"She'll understand."
"Will she, though?"
"Would you recognize her friend if you saw her walking alone in the mall?"

Silence, followed by laughter, and finally relief.

We talked ourselves in circles trying to justify a decision that didn't need justification. The truth had been sitting in the room the whole time; we just needed permission to say it out loud. The discussion wasn't about the party at all.

In that moment, we realized how often we force ourselves into motion, frequently overriding our own needs because we don't want to disappoint someone else. When we finally checked in with ourselves and not the expectations, the guilt, or the social scripts, the answer was simple:

We needed rest.
We needed quiet.
We needed permission to honor what our minds and bodies were already telling us.

That clarity, found only in the pause, allowed us to proceed with purpose. We politely declined the invitation, and more importantly, we released the guilt we were carrying about it. What seemed small at the time became a profound reminder: intention is not found in the rush, it's found in the stillness. With the decision not to attend the party, we were able to move forward from a place of alignment; we chose ourselves.

Sometimes the most intentional thing you can do is tell the truth to yourself first, and then to others.

"No."

No explanation.
No overthinking.
No guilt.

Proceeding with purpose means moving forward only in ways that honor your values. When your next step is rooted in intention, you no longer feel tugged in every direction. You walk with clarity. You choose with confidence. You lead with peace.

Purpose isn't found in the noise of constant activity; it is uncovered in the quiet courage to move differently.

 **KEY POINTS**

- Proceeding with intention brings peace, even in motion.

- A true yes is only possible when you honor your no.

REFLECTION QUESTIONS

- Where in your life are you currently moving out of habit rather than intention?

- What is one area where you feel called to slow down and realign your actions with your values?

- When was the last time you said yes out of guilt or obligation? What would an aligned choice have looked like?

08 Rest as Resistance

Reframing Rest

Rest is power. It is the conscious act of pausing, replenishing, and restoring your energy so that you can show up fully in every aspect of your life. **Scheduling rest intentionally is a declaration: I value my health, my focus, and my well-being.**

Rest can take many forms. It is not only sleep, even though that is fundamental. Rest can be as simple as reading a book, taking a walk, meditating, journaling, listening to music, or even sitting quietly with nothing on your agenda. The key is that rest is intentional and undistracted. It is a space to reset, reflect, and recharge.

Meeting with Myself

I used to resist rest. My calendar was packed, and any pause felt "unproductive." But everything changed when I began scheduling rest the way I would a meeting.

Each week, I block off dedicated time for a "meeting with myself." I rarely let anything override the scheduled meeting.

The time block is anywhere from 30 minutes to an hour and is dedicated to me to do whatever I deem necessary for that week. Sometimes I use the time to review my schedule for the upcoming week, which is a necessary part of my weekly self-care plan. Occasionally, I reflect on the previous month and highlight my accomplishments. I may even use the time to double down on a project or work task. Most often, though, I dedicate the time to prioritizing rest. I shut down my computer, sit quietly in my office, and do breathing exercises or listen to one of my favorite playlists. Occasionally, I run a few errands, giving myself a peaceful transition into post-work life.

At first, it felt uncomfortable, and I even felt guilty. However, over time, I've become more focused during work, more present with loved ones, and more in tune with my own needs. My creativity has increased, my stress has decreased, and my body finally feels like it was being heard.

I learned that when I embrace rest as a non-negotiable part of life, I am actively resisting the pressures of constant busyness and giving myself grace.

By making rest intentional and non-negotiable, you protect your mental and physical health, and you reclaim control over your time, your energy, and your life.

Why Rest is Important
- **Mental Health:** Reduces stress, prevents burnout, and improves focus.
- **Recharge:** Rejuvenates your mind and body, helping you be more present for others.
- **Self-Preservation:** Rest is a necessity, not a selfish act. It ensures you have the resources to meet life's demands.

KEY POINTS

- Rest is your right, not your reward. You do not need to earn the time your body and mind require.

- Stillness is a powerful strategy. Pausing allows for clarity, renewed energy, and better decision-making.

✦ ——  **PAUSE PRACTICE** ——┐

Schedule Your "Me Time"
- Block off 30–60 minutes each week.
- Label the time block clearly in your calendar (e.g., "Me Time," "Rest Hour," or "Recharge").
- Use the time for whatever restores you: reading, journaling, meditating, or doing nothing.
- Honor, protect, and commit to it like a work meeting.

Micro-Breaks Throughout the Day
- Set a timer for 60–90 minutes as a work block.
- Pause for 2–5 minutes to stretch, breathe, or simply step away from your workspace.

Rest Journaling
- At the end of each week, write down:
  - How often did you pause intentionally?
  - What activities helped you feel restored?
  - How did your energy, mood, or focus shift when you honored rest?
- Reflect on patterns and adjust your upcoming week to protect more restorative time.

Transition Rituals
- Create routines to mark the end of work to signal your mind and body that it's time to shift to rest and recovery.
- Examples: close your computer, stretch, take a short walk, or run errands mindfully.

09 Grace for the Journey

Life often feels like a race, one where we push forward, striving for goals, managing responsibilities, and meeting expectations without stopping to breathe. We fill our calendars, check off tasks, and measure our worth by what we accomplish rather than by how we feel. In this rush, it is easy to lose touch with ourselves, to overlook the small joys, the quiet victories, and the lessons embedded in each experience. Yet, growth rarely happens in haste. True strength is cultivated not in constant motion, but in the pauses we allow ourselves. These are the spaces where we step back, breathe deeply, and simply exist. It is in these pauses that we notice what truly matters, reconnect with our values, and prepare ourselves to move forward with intention.

Growth Through thePause

Pausing is where transformation begins; it serves as an act of courage.

When we allow ourselves moments of stillness, we create space to reflect, heal, and reset. Pausing enables us to step out of the noise and distraction of our daily routines and examine life with greater clarity. In these moments, we can observe our patterns, acknowledge what is working, and gently confront what is no longer serving us.

The pause is also where resilience is built. It provides a buffer between challenge and reaction, allowing us to respond rather than react impulsively. It is in this quiet space that lessons are absorbed, insights emerge, and we cultivate the wisdom to navigate life's complexities.

Practicing Gratitude and Forgiveness

Grace is a practice, one that begins with gratitude. Gratitude is more than a fleeting feeling; it is a conscious choice to notice the good, however small, that exists in each day. It might be the warmth of morning sunlight, a kind word from a colleague, or simply the ability to breathe deeply without discomfort. When we cultivate gratitude, we shift our perspective from scarcity to abundance, from lack to appreciation.

This shift allows us to see the beauty and progress in our lives, even amidst challenges, and reminds us that every small step forward is meaningful.

Equally important is forgiveness, especially toward ourselves. Life is imperfect, and so are we. We make mistakes, fall short of expectations, and sometimes fail to meet our own standards. Extending grace is the acknowledgment that growth is not linear, that setbacks are part of the journey, and that self-criticism does not define our worth. When we forgive ourselves, we lighten the burden we carry and make space for healing, reflection, and renewed effort.

Together, gratitude and forgiveness form the foundation of grace. By pausing, reflecting, and practicing these acts, we learn that growth does not come from relentless motion, but from the mindful moments where we breathe and permit ourselves to simply be.

Grace in Goal Setting

A few months ago, I sat down to plan my week. I identified three main priorities that I wanted to accomplish: tasks that were important for my work, my personal life, and my growth. I was determined to get everything crossed off my list, holding myself to the expectation that completing all three would define my success that week.

Midway through the week, life happened. A meeting ran long, a family obligation required my attention, and my energy was at an all-time low after several demanding days.

By Thursday, I realized that one of the three tasks was still untouched. My first instinct was frustration; I felt like I had failed, like I hadn't measured up to my own standards.

Then I paused. I reminded myself that the purpose of goal setting is not to create a tool for self-criticism but to guide focus and intention. I practiced grace: I acknowledged what I had accomplished, celebrated the two tasks I had completed, and forgave myself for the one that remained.

That small act of self-compassion changed everything. Rather than ending the week with guilt and regret, I felt a sense of calm and perspective. I had moved forward meaningfully, even if not perfectly.

By extending grace to myself, I learned that progress matters more than perfection and that every pause, every reflection, and every choice to forgive yourself builds resilience and strength.

From that week onward, I approached my goal-setting differently.

I still identify key priorities, but I also build in space for flexibility and self-compassion.

If something doesn't get crossed off your to-do list, it is not failure; it is an opportunity to reset, reflect, and adjust.

Grace, in this way, becomes an active part of progress, allowing us to move forward without carrying unnecessary weight.

Extending grace, both inward and outward, is not a one-time act but a continuous practice. Grace reminds us that the journey was never meant to be perfect. It was meant to be lived slowly, intentionally, and with compassion. And from here, we pause not to stop, but to move forward whole. It transforms the journey, turning challenges into opportunities for growth and slowing down into a source of strength. By embracing grace, we learn to move through life with compassion for ourselves and others, finding peace and progress in every step of the journey.

When we practice grace within ourselves, the pause naturally expands beyond us, influencing how we lead, connect, and show up in community.

REFLECTION QUESTIONS

- What would it look like to give yourself grace this week?

- How can gratitude and forgiveness shape the way you approach challenges and relationships?

- How can you extend grace when your plans or goals don't unfold perfectly?

Living in the Pause

❝

*Sometimes the fix is simple: pause, unplug,
and let yourself restart.*

10 The Pause in Community

> *"Almost everything will work again if you unplug it for a few minutes, including you."*
> Anne Lamott

Calm is not quiet.
Calm is leadership.

As leaders, whether in classrooms, offices, teams, or within our families, we teach far more through what we model than what we say. People notice how we move through challenges, how we respond in urgency, and how we care for ourselves while caring for others.

When we model intentional pauses, we give everyone around us permission to slow down, breathe, and reset.

This is the ripple effect of calm leadership: it shifts the energy of the entire space.

There's a special kind of magic that happens when people pause together.

Not a surface-level break, but a shared slowing down, an intentional stillness where everyone steps out of the rhythm of "go, go, go" and settles into something quieter, calmer, and more connected. I learned this deeply over the past year through a new adventure my husband and I discovered almost by accident.

What began as a simple weekend getaway with one of my cousins eleven years ago has grown into one of the most meaningful shifts in our relationship. That first "let's just try this" camping experience in New Braunfels set everything in motion. We bought the basics, including an air mattress and a tent, and headed out with zero expectations and open minds.

From that first tent to a Star Craft pop-up camper, a Gulf Stream Vintage Cruiser bumper pull trailer, and now dreams of a fifth wheel toy hauler in the near future, we've grown right alongside our camping journey. Last year alone, we took five trips, and we're already planning this year's list of adventures.

Every time we go, something in us exhales. Being out there in nature, everything feels different. The real power is in the stillness we've found together.

No deadlines. No overflowing calendar. No constant stream of notifications.

Sometimes the internet barely works, which honestly might be the biggest blessing of all. Instead, there's fresh air, trees taller than our worries, stars that make you pause mid-sentence, and coffee that somehow tastes better when sipped slowly on a park bench in the quiet morning air.

When we are camping, we breathe differently, talk differently, and even think differently. Nature has a way of slowing down just enough to hear your own thoughts again.

Pausing alone is powerful, but pausing together is transformative. The most meaningful shift hasn't been the scenery; it's been our collective focus on practicing our pause. The shared pause changed our dynamic. We connected in ways the busyness of home rarely allows. We had uninterrupted conversations. We laughed more. We moved at the same pace. Even within the silence, there is an increased connection.

This practice is also true for teams, groups, and families: **when you pause together, you recalibrate together**. You see each other more clearly. You understand more deeply. You make room for grace.

✦ ───  **PAUSE PRACTICE** ───┐

A shared moment of silence can be a powerful practice before decision-making, during conflict resolution, or as a way to gently close out the day. This intentional pause allows emotions to settle, thoughts to slow, and everyone to arrive fully in the present moment.

- Set a timer for five minutes.

- Invite everyone to find a comfortable position, whether seated or standing, with their feet grounded and bodies at ease.

- As a group, sit in silence. No talking, no phones, no multitasking. This is a protected space for stillness, reflection, and collective breathing.

- When the timer ends, transition slowly back into conversation. Invite each person to share one word that describes how they feel in that moment. Remind the team that there is no need to explain or justify the word; simply naming it is enough.

This practice often brings clarity, connection, and a shared sense of relief before moving forward together, supporting thoughtful decision-making, reducing emotional reactivity, and fostering a culture of presence and mutual respect.

REFLECTION QUESTIONS

- How can you invite others to join you in the pause?

  - Think of a team, group, or family you lead or influence.
  - What would a shared pause look like in that space?
  - Could it be a morning grounding moment?
  - A few deep breaths before beginning a conversation or meeting?
  - A ritual of stepping outside, stretching, or simply being quiet together?

- Consider one intentional way you can model the pause and one simple invitation you can extend to help others experience it with you.

_____

_____

_____

_____

_____

_____

11 From Practice to Lifestyle

" Transformation happens through small, consistent choices made over time."

The goal of this journey was never perfection, it was sustainability. Pausing, breathing, and proceeding were not meant to be tools you reach for only in moments of crisis, exhaustion, or a last resort. These small consistent practices are meant to become part of your daily rhythm, woven gently into the way you live, lead, and care for yourself.

Self-care is not indulgent or optional; it is essential. It is the practice of caring for yourself so that you can be healthy, do your work with integrity, support others, and meet the demands of your day with clarity and presence. Self-care encompasses the intentional actions we take to support our physical, mental, and emotional well-being, which encompasses everything from hygiene and nutrition to movement, sleep, reflection, mindfulness, connection, and seeking medical care when necessary.

In environments where productivity and achievement are often prioritized, especially in fields focused on outcomes, performance, and measurable results, self-care can feel difficult to justify. Yet it is precisely in these spaces that self-care becomes most necessary. When we care for ourselves consistently, we are better equipped to manage daily stressors, respond thoughtfully, and sustain our energy over time.

Establishing balance doesn't require drastic changes or additional hours in the day. Effective self-care is built through consistency and routine reflection. Just as we monitor our nutrition, hydration, sleep, and physical activity, we must also tend to our mental and emotional health through rest, relaxation, mindfulness, creativity, and meaningful relationships. There is no universal prescription for self-care; what matters is developing habits that are sustainable, intentional, and aligned with your needs.

Transformation does not require dramatic change or constant effort. It unfolds quietly through awareness, intention, and presence woven into everyday life. A single breath before responding, a moment of stillness between tasks, or a conscious decision to move with clarity instead of urgency can shift how you experience your day. These practices do not demand more from you; they invite you to live differently within what already exists.

Over time, pausing becomes instinctive, breathing becomes grounding, and proceeding with intention becomes a natural rhythm rather than a deliberate effort.

When pausing becomes a practice, it reshapes how you move through your day. You notice your body's cues sooner. You respond instead of react. Your breath becomes more than automatic; it becomes a bridge back to yourself. Proceeding no longer feels forced; it feels aligned.

One of the most powerful truths of this work is that the pause is always available to you. You don't need special conditions, extra time, or perfect circumstances. You can pause in the middle of a conversation, between meetings, before sending a message, or while standing in line. The pause meets you exactly where you are.

As these practices become habits, they stop feeling like something you do and start becoming who you are. You become someone who listens inward before responding outward. Someone who honors rest without guilt. Someone who moves forward with intention, even in the midst of a busy life.

Practice becomes a lifestyle, not through intensity, but through consistency. Not by doing more, but by being present more often.

Each time you choose to pause, breathe, and proceed with awareness, you reinforce a way of being that supports your well-being long-term.

# KEY POINTS

- Consistency over intensity sustains transformation.

- The pause is not a one-time act, it's a way of being.

✦ PAUSE PRACTICE

Before you turn the page, allow yourself one final intentional pause.

Sit comfortably.
If it feels safe, close your eyes or soften your gaze.
Take a slow breath in through your nose.
Hold gently at the top.
Release fully through your mouth.

Do that two more times, unrushed, unforced.

As you breathe, remind yourself:
I do not have to earn rest.
I do not have to justify slowing down.
I am allowed to move forward with intention.

Let this breath be a marker, not an ending, but a continuation. The practices in this book are not meant to live on these pages alone. They are meant to travel with you into meetings, conversations, classrooms, homes, relationships, and quiet moments you haven't yet imagined.

As a reminder, the pause is not something you arrive at once and master forever. It is something you return to, again and again, whenever life pulls you forward too quickly.

The Power Within the Pause

This journey has been about more than tips or routines; it's been about cultivating a deeper connection with yourself. From listening to your body and honoring its messages, to embracing rest as a radical act of self-respect, to extending grace in moments of imperfection, every chapter has invited you to slow down, reflect, and reclaim your energy.

Life will always present challenges, deadlines, and demands. The practices shared in these pages, listening to your body, nourishing yourself mindfully, resting intentionally, and cultivating gratitude and forgiveness, serve as guides for facing life's challenges with resilience, clarity, and compassion. They remind you that progress is not measured solely by productivity, that your worth is not contingent on constant achievement, and that slowing down is a strategy.

The pause is where transformation begins. In stillness, you hear your body, your heart, and your intuition. In reflection, you find clarity and alignment. In grace, you release the weight of perfection and embrace the journey as it unfolds.

The Power Within the Pause

As you move forward, remember this: self-care is not a luxury. Rest is not optional. Your body, mind, and spirit are your most precious resources, and honoring them is an act of courage, wisdom, and love.

May you carry these lessons into your daily life, permitting yourself to pause, to breathe, to reflect, and to extend grace to yourself and to others.

Life is not a race.
It is a journey.
The power to navigate it fully, with intention and joy, lives in your hands.

"In the pause, we find clarity.
In the breath, we find peace.
And in each intentional step forward,
we discover the life we were always
meant to live."

DR. MARCIE STRAHAN

About the Author

Dr. Marcie Strahan is a native Houstonian, an educational leader, speaker, and wellness advocate with over 30 years of experience dedicated to cultivating environments where students and adults can truly thrive. Throughout her career, she has held a variety of roles, including teacher, coach, counselor, assistant principal, principal, and district-level administrator.

Currently serving as the Executive Director of Mental Health and School Support, Dr. Strahan designs and supports systems that center on resilience, intentional care, and sustainable leadership practices. Her work bridges education, mental health, and mindful living, grounded in the belief that true success requires balance, self-trust, and rest.

Dr. Strahan is the author of Self-Care Workbook: 52 Week Goal-Setting, Weekly Reflection Journal, and Activities Focusing on Personal Well-Being and Threads of Sisterhood: A Journal of Gratitude and Reflection. Through her guided practices, she invites readers to explore emotional, mental, physical, practical, social, and spiritual self-care while nurturing gratitude as a daily practice.

She is also a contributing author to Shattering Stereotypes: Fiercely Forging Forward, a collection of stories highlighting individuals who have challenged limitations and redefined success on their own terms.

In 2024, Dr. Strahan launched SHIFT Matters, LLC to expand her mission beyond school walls. Through this work, she supports individuals, teams, and leaders in strengthening wellness, resilience, and productivity through purposeful, values-aligned action. She holds a Doctorate in Professional Leadership from the University of Houston.

At the heart of her work is a simple yet transformative message: when we honor our well-being, we show up more fully in our work, our relationships, and our purpose. Dr. Strahan is passionate about helping others pause, reflect, and reconnect with what matters most. She firmly believes that healing, growth, and grace begin when we slow down.

Speaking Engagements

Dr. Strahan's passion is helping educators and leaders protect their well-being, strengthen their resilience, and cultivate healthy, sustainable habits. She speaks from lived experience and professional expertise, combining her deep knowledge of social-emotional learning with her compassionate leadership approach.

Audiences walk away with practical strategies, renewed motivation, and a deeper understanding that caring for themselves is not optional; it's essential. Dr. Strahan's message reminds us: when we pause on purpose, we rise with intention. For more information, availability, and pricing, email marcie@marciestrahan.com.

Supporting Articles & Resources

- American Psychological Association, 2019; Brandani et al., 2017; Hopper et al., 2019; Jerath et al., 2015; Russo et al., 2017; Saoji et al., 2019; Zaccaro et al., 2018.

- HelpGuide.org. (n.d.). The benefits of mindfulness. https://www.helpguide.org/mental-health/stress/benefits-of-mindfulness

- Prevention. (n.d.). How to relieve stress — 28 science-backed ways to relax. Prevention. Retrieved from https://www.prevention.com/health/mental-health/g26542035/how-to-relieve-stress/

- Yoga Journal. (2026). The Power of Mindfulness. Yoga Journal. Retrieved from https://www.yogajournal.com

Made in the USA
Coppell, TX
24 February 2026

72720914R00056